Best Motoring Jokes

OTHER TITLES IN THIS SERIES:

Best Jewish Jokes
Best Irish Jokes
Best Scottish Jokes
Best Animal Jokes
Best Psychiatric Jokes
Best Salesmen's Jokes
Best Medical Jokes
Best Mother-in-Law Jokes
Best Religious Jokes
Best Drinking Jokes
Best Golfing Jokes
The World's Worst Jokes
The World's Worst Riddles
The Morecambe and Wise Joke Book
The World's Worst Puns
Best Schoolboy Jokes
Best Army Jokes
Best Football Jokes
Best Newly-wed Jokes
Michael Howard's Best Shaggy Dog Stories
More Best Irish Jokes
More Best Jewish Jokes
Best Irish Limericks
Best Howlers
Best Yorkshire Jokes
Best Lancashire Jokes
Best West Country Jokes
Best Seaside Jokes
The Mike and Bernie Winters' Joke Book
Best Ulster Jokes
Best Nursing Jokes
Best Fishing Jokes
Best Australian Jokes

THE WOLFE MINI HA-HA BOOKS

BEST Motoring JOKES

by Colin Crompton

WOLFE PUBLISHING LTD
10 EARLHAM STREET LONDON WC2

SBN 72340419 4

Printed by Oxley Press Limited, Nottingham.

Introduction

WELL, I incurred the wrath of the ladies when I had a light-hearted laugh at them in *Best Newly-Wed Jokes* and I'm very much afraid that the same thing will happen when they read this book which contains a good share of 'woman driver' and 'back-seat driver' jokes!

This was inevitable, because I have tried to cover every aspect of motoring from buying a car to wrecking it—and let's be honest, girls, the book would have been incomplete if you hadn't been included. I read somewhere that the part of a car which causes most accidents is the nut behind the wheel. It didn't say whether it was a male nut or a female nut, but I have a sneaking suspicion that there are the same proportion of each.

'Back-seat drivers' are a menace, of course—if they really exist. I may have been lucky, but I've never come across one and am inclined to think that they are an invention of script-writers. ('How did the accident happen?' 'My wife fell asleep in the back seat.')

It's safe to assume that you're not driving as you read this (you're *not*, are you?) so you can enjoy reading about the stupid things that drivers do. *Other* drivers, naturally.

And a last word to the ladies: I'll take the high road, and you take the low road. Please.

Colin Crompton

When a woman driver puts her hand out of the window she is going to turn left, turn right, reverse, or stop. Or she may be waving at someone. Or drying her nail varnish. In fact, the only thing you can be sure of is that the window is open.

A Post Office engineer was climbing a telegraph pole as a woman motorist drove by.

'Look at that idiot,' she said to her passenger. 'You'd think I'd never driven a car before.'

'How is your wife getting on with her driving lessons?'

'Fine. The road is beginning to turn now when she does.'

'Don't you know this is a one-way street?'

'That's okay. I'm only going one way.'

Policeman (to man driving past a 'Halt' sign): 'Hey, can't you read?'

Motorist: 'Yes, I can read, but I can't stop.'

The nervous motorist stalled his engine at some traffic lights and frantically tried to restart it as the lights changed from red, through amber, to green, and back again.

A policeman watched this performance for several minutes before strolling across and asking, 'What's the matter? Haven't we got a colour that suits you?'

Wife (tearfully): 'I tried to turn the corner.'

Husband: 'Well, what happened?'

Wife: 'I was in the middle of the block.'

'Now, miss, what gear were you in at the time of the accident?'

'Oh, I was wearing a red mini-skirt, a white blouse and a yellow cardigan.'

'Why on earth did you run into a policeman?'

'It was the best way I knew to sober up.'

Two pedestrians were knocked down by a car driven by a young lady.

'Did you get her number?' asked one.

'No,' replied the other. 'How could I get her number when she was going so fast?'

'Nice-looking girl, though, wasn't she?'

'Yes. Did you see her beautiful blue eyes?'

'How did he come to lose control of his car at the level-crossing?'

'He's an ardent trade-unionist. Drops everything when the whistle blows.'

'Have an accident?'

'No thanks—I've just had one.'

'How did you come to have an accident with that car that I sold you?'

'I couldn't put my hand out while I was pushing it round the corner.'

'It was the motor-cyclist's fault, officer. He had so many rear-view mirrors on his machine that he couldn't see where he was going, and he hit my front wing.'

'What's happened to your speedometer?'

'I didn't need it, so I took it out and sold it.'

'Didn't need it? How can you manage without it?'

'Easy. At 20 mph the exhaust rattles, at 30 mph the door rattles, and at 40 mph I rattle.'

Driving Instructor (to lady stalled at traffic lights): 'Use your noodle, madam, use your noodle!'

Lady Driver: 'Well, where is it, then? I've pushed and pulled everything else on the dashboard.'

'Hey, you're blocking up the traffic! Can't you go any faster?'
'Yes, but I don't want to leave the car.'

'Isn't it dangerous to drive a car with one hand?'
'Yes. Many a young man has run into a church by doing it.'

Magistrate: 'The officer says that you were driving at 80 miles an hour on the wrong side of the road, in the middle of the night without any lights on. What have you got to say?'

Motorist: 'It was necessary, Your Worship. The car was stolen.'

'I got rid of that noise in the back of my car.'
'Oh? How?'
'I made her sit in the front with me.'

'Do you know that you were travelling at 50 mph?'
'Impossible. I've only been out for twenty minutes.'

At last I've discovered the reason for the amber light in traffic lights. It gives Scots motorists the chance to start their engines.

'I'm going to buy a car.'
'Why?'
'I've just found a parking-place.'

They were driving along a quiet country lane when he said, 'You look lovelier every minute. Do you know what that's a sign of?'

'Yes,' replied the pretty blonde passenger. 'You're about to run out of petrol.'

Salesman (demonstrating car): 'Now I will throw in the clutch.'

Farmer's Boy: 'I'll buy her, then. I knew if I held out long enough you'd give me something for nothing.'

They were talking about cross-breeding in the local when the bored landlord said, 'I once crossed a bridge with a car.'

'Amazing! What was the result?'

'I got to the other side.'

The man was lying on the zebra crossing when the policeman dashed up and shouted, 'Where's the car that hit him? Did somebody get its number?'

The man rose to his feet and said, 'Wait a minute, officer. I was trying to cross on the zebra crossing when a driver stopped and motioned me to go over. The shock was too much, and I fainted.'

A pedestrian is a man with a wife, a daughter, two sons and a car.

Heard outside a public-house: 'You drive, Tommy. You're too drunk to sing.'

'The way some pedestrians walk, you'd think they owned the roads.'

'Yes, and the way some motorists drive, you'd think they owned their cars.'

'Mummy, what happens to a car when it gets so old that it won't go?'

'Somebody sells it to your father and says it's as good as new.'

'You sold me this car two weeks ago.'

'Yes, sir.'

'Tell me again all that you said about it before I bought it. I'm getting discouraged.'

'How much will it cost to have my car repaired?'

'What's wrong with it?'

'I haven't the slightest idea.'

'Twenty-two pounds, ten shillings and ninepence.'

'Didn't you guarantee when you sold me this car that you would replace anything that broke?'

'That's correct, sir.'

'Well, I want a new garage door.'

'You'd never think that this car was second-hand, would you?'

'No. It looks as if you made it yourself.'

Patrolman (straightening up from open bonnet of lady's car): 'The point is, madam, that your battery's flat.'

Lady driver (brightly): 'Oh, is it? What shape should it be?'

'Has your wife learnt to drive the car yet?'

'Yes, in an advisory capacity.'

'Why are you racing through town at 60 mph?'

'Well you see, officer, my brakes aren't working and I want to get home before there's an accident.'

'That girl I took out driving last night was a witch.'

'Good heavens! How did you find out?'

'She put her hand on my knee and I turned into a lay-by.'

Then there's the girl who spends so much time in parked cars that the motoring organisations show her on route maps.

'You went the wrong way round that traffic island. Didn't you see the arrows?'

'Arrows? I didn't even see the Indians.'

'What's the best thing to do if the brakes on your car fail?'

'Hit something cheap.'

A motorist was unable to avoid hitting a rather fat woman, but she got up unhurt and demanded angrily, 'Why didn't you go round me?'

'Because I didn't have enough petrol,' retorted the motorist.

Attendant: 'Is four gallons enough, sir?'

Motorist: 'Yes, thank you.'

Attendant: 'Check your oil, sir?'

Motorist: 'No, thank you. It's okay.'

Attendant: 'Got enough water in your radiator?'

Motorist: 'Yes, it's full.'

Attendant: 'Battery need topping up?'

Motorist: 'No, thank you.'

Attendant: 'Anything else, sir?'

Motorist: 'Yes, would you please stick your tongue out so that I can seal this letter?'

Driving Instructor: 'Now, madam, this is the gear lever; down there is the clutch on the left; next to it, in the middle, is the brake; and next to that, on the right, is the accelerator.'

Lady: 'Just a minute! Let's take one thing at a time. Teach me to drive first.'

He was rather foolishly having a little sleep while his wife was driving.

He was rudely awakened by her shouting, 'Tell me, George, quick! Which is the right side of the road to keep on when you're running down a hill backwards like this?'

'Where do you think you're going?' the policeman asked the driver who was going the wrong way up a one-way street.
'I don't know,' the driver replied. 'But it can't be much good. Everyone's coming back.'

'How's your brakes?'
'You should worry. It's my car.'

The pretty young girl raised no objection as her new boy-friend stopped his car in a secluded lay-by, but said 'No' when he suggested that she move on to the back seat. Some twenty minutes later, after some passionate kissing, he again asked her to move into the back, but again she refused.
The result was the same when he asked her again after another kissing session in which she was a most willing partner.
'Why on earth not?' he demanded.
'Because I want to stay in the front with you,' she replied.

'Don't you ever take your wife out with you in the car?'
'No. I can't contend with both of them together.'

A car full of drunks was proceeding erratically down the street when it was stopped by a policeman on a motor-cycle.
'Now then,' said the arm of the law. 'Who's the driver?'
'Got you there, offisher,' said one of the occupants. 'We were all in the back.'

A policeman was standing on the crowded car-park of a public-house at closing time. Among the people coming out, he spotted one man who was very unsteady on his feet. He watched as the man staggered to a car, fell over the bonnet, straightened himself up, fumbled for his keys and—after about five minutes—managed to open the car door. As he flopped into the driving seat and was about to insert the ignition key, the policeman went over to him and asked him his name, address and occupation.

The man got out of the car, observed the now-empty car-park and said, 'Officer, I am a tee-totaller. My name is Reginald Barkley. My address is No. 1, The Elms. And I am a professional decoy.'

Statistics show that one man gets knocked down by a car in London every three hours. And he's getting tired of it.

'I need a longer dip-stick in my car.'

'Why, madam?'

'The one that's in won't reach the oil.'

'Are you drunk?' the policeman asked the man he found lying flat on his back in the gutter.

'No.'

'Well, what are you doing flat on your back in the gutter, then?'

'I've found a parking space, and I've sent the wife home for the car.'

Mechanic (repairing an old, broken-down car): 'You've got a good horn here, Mister. Why don't you jack it up and run a car under it?'

Husband: 'Why are you crouched over the wheel like that?'

Wife: 'Didn't you see that sign we just passed? It said "Bend for two miles".'

Policeman (producing notebook): 'Name, please.'

Motorist: 'Aloysius Alistair Cyprian de Willoughby-Smythe.'

Policeman (putting book away): 'Well, don't let me catch you again.'

'What did your husband say when you smashed the new car?'

'Shall I leave out the four-letter swear words?'

'Yes.'

'He didn't say a thing.'

Wife (learning to drive): 'I don't know what to do.'

Husband: 'Just imagine I'm driving.'

Police Sergeant: 'Did you catch the man driving that stolen car?'

Constable: 'No, he was dead lucky. I was within fifty yards of him when my mileage reached 5,000 and I had to stop and have the oil changed.'

A visitor was being shown round a mental hospital and visited a room which he was told was reserved for 'car maniacs'.

'But the room is empty,' observed the visitor. 'Are there no patients?'

'Yes,' said his guide. 'They're all under their beds repairing the springs.'

'Why is your car painted blue on one side and red on the other?'

'I like to hear the witnesses contradicting each other.'

It's funny that a woman who can spot a blonde hair on your coat at ten paces can't see a pair of garage doors.

Hell, for garage mechanics, will be a land of abundant grease and no steering-wheels to wipe it on.

A miss in the car is worth two in the engine.

Magistrate, 1990: 'Wrong side of the cloud, eh? Fined £500 and costs.'

'I turned the way that I signalled,' said the lady indignantly, after the crash.

'I know,' retorted the man. 'That's what fooled me.'

Radio Announcer: 'The police are keeping Bank Holiday traffic moving slowly and by mid-afternoon, when they have more men on point duty, they hope to be able to bring it to a complete standstill.'

'It's absurd for this man to charge £5 for towing us two miles.'

'That's all right—he's earning it. I've got my brakes on.'

Policeman: 'You were driving at 75 mph, miss.'

She: 'Isn't that marvellous! And I only passed my test yesterday.'

Woman Driver: 'Can you fix this bumper so that my husband will never know that I bent it?'

Mechanic: 'No, but I can fix it so that you can ask him in a few days how *he* bent it.'

'What model is Alf's car?'

'It's not a model—it's a horrible example.'

Policeman: 'How did the accident happen?'

Motorist: 'My wife fell asleep in the back seat.'

When people joked about Ford cars: Henry Ford, who believed in using his own cars, was in the suburbs of Detroit one day when he saw the driver of a Ford car trying to start the engine. Ford got out of his own car, helped the other motorist and, in a few minutes, the stalled car was ready to run again. The grateful owner pulled out half a dollar and offered it to Ford. The money was declined with the statement, 'I have more money than I can find any use for, and I was only too glad that I was able to get your car started for you.'

The man looked at Ford and then at Ford's car, and said with emphasis, 'You're a liar. If you had more money than you knew what to do with, you wouldn't be running a b—Ford.'

A woman motorist posed for a snapshot in front of the fallen pillars of an ancient temple in Greece.

'Don't get the car in the picture,' she warned, 'or my husband will think I ran into the place.'

'I haven't seen John for months.'

'Haven't you heard? He got three years for stealing a car.'

'The fool. Why didn't he buy one and not pay for it, like a gentleman?'

I never stall my car in the middle of dense traffic.
I never get a puncture a week after I've bought a new tyre.
I never run out of petrol five miles from a garage.
I never have any trouble finding a parking place.
I never get a ticket from a traffic-warden.
I haven't got a car.

Vicar: 'I'm returning that second-hand car which I bought from you last week.'
Dealer: 'What's wrong? Can't you run it?'
Vicar: 'Not and stay in the ministry.'

Breathes there a man with soul so dead
Who never to a cop has said,
When over the limit he has sped,
'Why don't you pinch that car ahead?'

Girl: 'For goodness sake, use both hands.'
Boy: 'I can't. I have to steer with one.'

'Do you know how to drive a car?'
'I thought I did until I had a short talk with a policeman yesterday.'

Statistics prove that railway trains are not afraid of cars.

Motorist: 'Want a lift.'
Hiker: 'No thanks. I'm walking for exercise.'
Motorist: 'Exercise? What's that?'

'Does this petrol stop knocking?'
'Yes.'
'Then fill the wife up.'

FIFTEEN COMMANDMENTS FOR MOTORISTS

1. The policeman is always right. Don't contradict him.

2. Never crowd a lorry on to the curb.

3. Never contradict a policeman.

4. Never run over a traffic policeman's foot.

5. Never contradict a policeman.

6. Drive round bollards in the middle of the road.

7. Never contradict a policeman.

8. Always give a woman enough room to change her mind.

9. Never contradict a policeman.

10. Try to avoid running into a mounted policeman's horse.

11. Never contradict a policeman.

12. Always plead guilty in court.

13. Never contradict a policeman.

14. Never try to beat a fire engine at traffic lights. Picking you up will delay the firemen.

15. Never contradict a policeman.

Magistrate: 'You are charged with running over a man, and also speeding.'

Motorist: 'Yes. I was hurrying to get over him.'

'Your car's at the front door, sir.'

'I know. I can hear it knocking.'

She: 'Can you drive with one hand?'

He: 'I should say so!'

She: 'Then wipe your nose, it's running.'

A lot of car crashes are caused by tight nuts.

Policeman (in restaurant): 'Your car awaits without.'

Diner: 'Without what?'

Policeman: 'Without lights. Name and address, please.'

'How are your brakes?'

'They're a scream!'

Motto for motorists: 'Don't blast your horn until you can see the whites of their eyes.'

He: 'If I drove with my right hand, would it annoy you?'

She: 'No, but your left hand probably would.'

Women who drive from the back seat are no worse than men who cook from the dining-room table.

'Can your wife drive?'
'She's had ten lessons and knows how to aim.'

'The brakes on this car are so good that you can be travelling at 100 mph and stop in five yards.'

'What happens then?'

'A putty knife comes out automatically and scrapes you off the windscreen.'

'That's a big car. Aren't you afraid of losing control of it?'
'Constantly. I'm three instalments behind already.'

He: 'Do you want a lift, love?'
She: 'No thanks. I'm just walking back from one.'

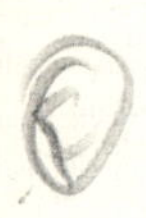

A motor-car manufacturer designed a completely new 'car of the future' and advertised for a motorist who would drive it for six months and give it a thorough testing.

The successful applicant sat in the driving seat of the car, and the designer sat next to him in the passenger seat.

'You'll find this car to be completely different from anything that you have ever driven before,' said the designer. 'There is no engine, no battery, no gears, no accelerator, no brake. In fact, there's nothing to go wrong at all. The only mechanism —if you can describe it as such—is a small black box, no bigger than a match-box, which is located under the driving-seat. It is, in fact, an electronic computer which reacts to the sound waves it receives from the driver's voice. It has the added advantage that it can be set to receive code words of the driver's own choice, thus making it impossible for anybody to steal the car. Now—to make the car go—all you have to say is, "Flippin' 'eck", because we've set it for that at the factory.'

So the driver said, 'Flippin' 'eck' and the car started to move forward.

'How do I make it stop?' he asked.

'By the same principal,' answered the designer. 'Just say "Hocus Pocus".'

So the driver said, 'Hocus Pocus' and the car stopped. He tried it a dozen times and it never failed. 'Flippin' 'eck' and the car moved forward, 'Hocus Pocus' and it stopped.

After driving the car round for several weeks, he took his girl-friend to the coast in it, and she was very impressed. As night was falling, she whispered to him in a romantic voice, 'Let's stop on the edge of that cliff; there's a lovely view.'

Nearing the cliff edge, the driver said, 'Hocus Pocus', but nothing happened.

'Hocus Pocus!' he shouted, but the car still moved forward towards the cliff edge and a sheer drop into the sea.

'Hocus Pocus!' he screamed, and the car stopped about an inch from the edge of the cliff.

Breathing a sigh of relief, the driver said, 'Flippin' 'eck!'

'This car will go 300 miles without filling the petrol tank.'

'How far will it go if you put petrol in it?'

The advertisement for the Driving School read: 'Complete Course, £25'. Underneath, in small print, it said, 'Learn to fold roadmaps, £40 extra.'

'Do you like my new car? It's fully automatic and has a caravan on the back.'

'What do you want a caravan for?'

'I don't want it, but the hire purchase company has got a branch office in it.'

'She's in love with her car.'

'Yes. Another example of man being replaced by machinery.'

'But officer, I was speeding because I'm late for an appointment with my solicitor.'

'Well, now you've got something else to tell him about.'

Policeman: 'You were doing 50 mph.'

Motorist: 'Would you mind putting 80 mph on the summons? Then I can show it to the man I'm trying to sell this car to.'

Policeman: 'Don't you know what I mean when I hold my hand up?'

Lady Driver: 'I should do. I was a schoolteacher for fifteen years.'

Pretty Young Miss: 'I was out with a drunken driver last night and he headed straight for a telegraph pole.'

Witty Young Miss: 'The dog.'

'Is Fred a careful driver?'

'He must be. Every accident he's been in has been the other man's fault.'

'My brother commutes.'

'I thought he had a car.'

'He has. He commutes between the parking space and the office.'

'How did you come to be in hospital?'

'I was driving along at a steady 30 mph down the motorway, when a sports car overtook me. He was going so fast that I thought I'd stopped, and I got out.'

Boy: 'You'd feel better if you came for a drive in the country with me.'

Girl: 'Yes, I'm sure it would put me on my feet.'

Two men were in the changing-room at the golf club.

'Good heavens, old man!' said one. 'How long have you been wearing a girdle?'

'Ever since the wife found it in the glove compartment of the car,' sighed the other.

A pretty young girl went for a drive in the country with her boss from the office, and returned home with a muddy left shoe. She'd had second thoughts at the last minute.

'Did you get the number of the car that knocked you down?'
'No, but I'd recognise the driver's laugh anywhere.'

A girl doesn't have to watch the speedo to know what her boyfriend is driving at.

She: 'I'll give you a kiss and a cuddle if you'll take me for a drive in your new car.'
He: 'That's fare enough.'

The latest cars have the front bumper made of rubber so that, after you've hit somebody, it erases your licence number off the back of his pants.

'The brakes on this car are wonderful, sir. Instead of running over a pedestrian, you can stop right on top of him.'

'Why do you refer to your car as "she"?'
'Because it has beautiful curves, is not altogether trustworthy, and keeps me broke.'

It was midnight and the police car driver found himself behind a brand new car. He was pleased to notice that the driver didn't go over 28 or 29 mph and that, even though there was no traffic about, he signalled his every move, observed lane procedure, and generally impressed with his meticulous handling of the car. In fact, the policeman was so taken with the man's driving that he stopped him to congratulate him.

'I'm not booking you,' he said. 'I've stopped you to congratulate you on your wonderful driving. You're a model to all other road-users. If everybody drove like you, my job would be a lot easier.'

The driver looked up at the policeman and, with a glazed look in his eyes, said, 'Well, you've got to watch it when you've had a few, haven't you?'

'Why did he name his car after his wife?'

'Because he found out that he couldn't control it.'

'Charlie says he's going to have bigger wheels fitted to his mini-car.'

'Why?'

'Dogs keep wetting the windows.'

A woman motorist shouted 'Pig!' at a male driver who was travelling in the opposite direction along a narrow country lane.

The man wound his window down and retaliated by shouting, 'Old bat!' back.

Then he ran over a pig.

Fact: Just after the turn of the century a no-doubt worthy organisation called the Farmers' Anti-Automobile Society set itself up in America and published a pamphlet of 'rules' for motorists who drove on country lanes.

One rule suggested that a car owner, propelling his vehicle after dark, should stop every mile, send up a warning rocket, and then wait for ten minutes to ensure that the road ahead was clear before proceeding.

'If a horse is unwilling to pass an automobile,' the Society declared on another page, 'the driver should take the machine apart as rapidly as possible and conceal the parts in the bushes.'

Hitch-hiker: 'Have you got a radio in your car?'
Motorist: 'No.'
Hitch-hiker: 'Well, drive on then!'

A speeding car came to a screeching halt at a road junction, just missing a little old lady who, having the traffic lights in her favour, was walking from one side of the road to the other.

The old lady didn't appear to be either frightened or annoyed. She merely smiled at the driver, and pointed to a pair of baby shoes which were hanging from his rear-view mirror.

'Young man,' she demanded, 'why don't you put your shoes back on?'

An old American hill-billy came into a small and totally unexpected inheritance. He decided to buy a second-hand car to ease the burden of his declining years. The cheapest he could find was priced at more than the money he had, but the dealer said, 'You get five good tyres thrown in free.'

'Forget the tyres,' said the hill-billy. 'I don't want any on my car. When I'm driving, I want to know it.'

'Jones is so old-fashioned.'

'In what way?'

'He always stops when he hits another car.'

A young man called for his steady girl-friend to take her out for a drive in the country in his new car. As soon as they were out of the town, he pulled in the first lay-by they came to.

'Richard,' protested the young lady, 'why stop here on the main road where everyone can see us? There are some much nicer places farther on.'

'Here we are, and here we stay,' said the young man firmly. 'I believe in love at first site.'

The day after a sedate schoolteacher bought a second-hand car, she drove it back to the dealer's.

'What's wrong?' asked the dealer anxiously.

'Nothing at all,' replied the schoolteacher sweetly. 'I just want to return these things for the dear old lady you told me owned the car before you sold it to me. She left this pipe in the glove compartment, and this half-empty bottle of whisky under the seat.'

Nothing improves your driving like being followed by a police-car.

'What mileage you can get out of these new economy models,' boasted Mr. Newlywed on his return from his honeymoon trip. 'My bride and I had to stop at more garages than our car did.'

The League of Pedestrians is heartily in favour of shorter motor-cars. They say that when they run over you, they don't stay on you so long.

She: 'Be an angel and let me drive.'
He did—and he is.

A man took his car into a swank West End garage for a tune-up and was handed a bill for £50.
'Hey,' he protested, 'Who did this tune-up—Liberace?'

An old man was inching his dilapidated jalopy down the main street of the village when a policeman signalled him to halt.
'Don't worry, pop,' said the officer, reassuringly. 'I'm not pinching you for anything. I just wanted to see what it feels like to put my foot on a running-board again.'

Mrs. Smitherley-Smythe was tootling along quite happily at a steady 20 mph in the right-hand lane of a dual-carriageway when, without warning, she suddenly made a sharp left turn and collided with another car.

'Blank, Blank, Blank!' roared the other driver. 'Why the blank-blank didn't you signal?'

'Don't be absurd,' countered Mrs. Smitherley-Smythe loftily. 'I *always* turn here.'

A police-car flagged down a lady driver who had been doing eighty-five on a busy motorway and dodging from lane to lane.

He examined her licence and returned it to her with this quizzical observation: 'Your licence seems to be valid, madam. Now, would you mind telling me how the heck you got it?'

'Don't you know that you should always give half of the road to a woman driver?'

'I always do—when I find out which half of the road she wants.'

A fast sports car rounded a corner on two wheels, knocked down a policeman and half a dozen pedestrians, and finally wrapped itself round a telegraph pole.

A sweet young thing climbed out of the wreckage.

'Yippee!' she cried. 'That's what I call a kiss!'

A vicar ran out of petrol, but wasn't too despondent as the nearest garage was only fifty yards away. Then he realised that he hadn't got an empty can in which to carry the petrol.

Wondering what to do, he spotted the baby's 'potty' which his wife had left on the back seat of the car after a family picnic the previous day. 'That should hold half a gallon,' he thought, and set off with it for the garage.

He bought the petrol, carried it back in the 'potty', and was pouring it into his petrol tank when one of his parishioners came round the corner.

The man took in the scene at a glance and said, 'Good heavens, vicar, you've got more faith than I have.'

A policeman spotted a lady motorist who was calmly driving down the wrong side of the road. He stopped her and asked testily, 'Don't you know what the white line in the middle of the road is for?'

The lady considered carefully, and then hazarded, 'Bicycles?'

An elderly matron, driving a car of about the same age as herself, turned too sharply at a road junction and neatly ran over the left foot of a policeman directing traffic. His loud shout brought her to a stop. Helpfully, she put the car into reverse and backed towards the officer.

'I knew it!' he roared in anguish. 'Now you've got the other one!'

A Londoner drove up to the Midlands without incident but, once he reached the Birmingham area, he found himself hopelessly confused in the complex of new underpasses, overpasses, and roundabouts which had been built in connection with the junction of the M1, the M5, and the M6 motorways.

Finally, he pulled up alongside a man who had a woman and two children in the car with him.

'Can you help me out?' implored the Londoner. 'I've been trying to get on the Wolverhampton road for two hours, and I always finish up here.'

'You're asking the wrong man,' the other driver replied wearily. 'I haven't even got home from my honeymoon.'

A motorist stopped at a roadside snack-bar and ordered a cup of tea and a chocolate doughnut. A few moments after he had been served, he called over the woman who was in charge and said to her, 'I can tell you something about yourself. You have a small son who plays in the kitchen with a toy car.'

'You're absolutely right,' gasped the woman. 'You must be a mind-reader.'

'Not at all,' replied the motorist. 'Just put me down as the man you served a toy tyre to instead of a chocolate doughnut.'

'Haven't you got more sense than to leave that window open?' scolded your actual back seat driver. 'It's blowing my hair too much.'

'How far can a little wind blow your hair?' scoffed the driver.

'The last little bit,' she replied, 'blew it about three miles.'

The dizzy blonde gurgled happily: 'I had my first driving lesson today. I think I did very well, too. But, my goodness, that ignition key is tricky.'

Mrs. Heywood was explaining how her car had swerved off the road in the dark: 'I was following the white line, and the white line turned out to be a rabbit.'

A village lad couldn't get out of the way fast enough, and was struck amidships by a huge dog that came loping over the crest of a hill and catapulted him into a ditch. He struggled up and started to dust himself off when a girl in a tiny foreign sports car roared into view and knocked him down again.

'The dog didn't hurt me a bit,' he reported later. 'But the tin can tied to his tail nearly killed me.'

A businessman was sitting in his office coping with problems of commerce when he was interrupted by a telephone call from his eight-year-old son.

'Mummy ran over my bicycle when she was backing her car out of the garage this morning,' wailed the boy.

The unsympathetic father replied, 'How many times have I warned you not to leave your bicycle in the middle of the front lawn?'

The country squire was constantly annoyed by motorists who whizzed past his house at 70 mph. He finally put a stop to it with a large sign that slowed drivers down to a crawl.

The sign proclaimed: PLEASE PROCEED WITH CARE. NUDIST CAMP CROSSING JUST AHEAD.

'Have you ever been pinched for going too fast?'

'No, but I've been slapped.'

Old Harry, whose life had been far from blameless, died and arrived at the gates of Hell. The Devil checked his records and said, 'I see that your wife, your mother-in-law and your three daughters all passed their driving-test at their first attempt, and that you never managed to pass yours at all.'

'That's correct,' confirmed Harry.

'In that case,' said the Devil, 'you can go upstairs to Heaven. You've had enough hell on earth.'

Aunt Sarah grew somewhat eccentric in her declining years but, since the whole family hoped to inherit some of her considerable fortune, she was humoured in her every whim.

One afternoon, at the height of a thunderstorm, she decided that she would like a drive in her grandson's sports car—an open-roofed model. The young man dutifully escorted her to the car, climbed behind the wheel and, without moving from the garage, went through the motions of taking her for a drive.

After half-an-hour they re-entered the house and Aunt Sarah said, 'Rodney is quite a good driver, but I think he's just a little bit odd. There we were, driving through pouring rain in an open car, and he didn't put his hat on.'

The police car eventually stopped the young lady who was exceeding the speed limit in her sports car.

'Didn't you see me waving at you a mile back?' demanded the policeman.

'Of course,' pouted the girl. 'But I never flirt when I'm driving.'

A pessimist is a female who's afraid that she won't be able to squeeze her car into a very small parking space.

An optimist is a male who thinks she won't try.

You can always pick out the owner of a car in which four ladies are riding. She's the one who, after somebody shuts the door, always opens it and slams it harder.

Donald and his wife were driving from Stalybridge in Cheshire across the Pennines to Sheffield. It was the first time they had done the journey and Donald's wife had a map spread out on her lap.

'Slow up!' she suddenly exclaimed. 'You turn right on this road here.'

Donald turned right, but grumbled, 'I don't like the looks of this road.'

He liked it even less when it tailed off into a cowpath through a farm. Stopping the car he said, 'Let me look at that map.'

One glance was enough.

'That's not a road, my precious one,' he said. 'That is the county border line.'

The woman driver was tootling merrily through a village on the wrong side of the road and ran smack into a brand new car.

While they were trying to separate the two vehicles, the lady said reluctantly, 'I'm afraid it was my fault.'

'Nonsense,' said the man gallantly. 'I saw you coming fully a hundred yards away, and I had ample time to drive into the pond and avoid you.'

Two rival businessmen were continually trying to prove that each had more money than the other. They both had every conceivable status symbol, including the most expensive limousine on the market.

When one had a telephone installed in his car, the other did likewise and phoned his rival to let him know about it. But the rival had still kept one jump ahead. When the phone rang, a secretary leaned over from the passenger seat, answered it, and said, 'I'm afraid you can't speak to him now. He's on the other line.'

A woman was driving her car at about 60 miles an hour in a built-up area when she noticed in her rear-view mirror that a motor-cycle policeman was following her. Instead of slowing down, she thought that she could shake him off by increasing her speed to 70 miles an hour.

Looking through her mirror again, she saw that there were now two motor-cycle policemen following her. She stepped up her speed to 80 miles an hour and, when she looked again, there were three policemen on her tail.

Suddenly she saw a garage up ahead and, pulling into it, she got out and dashed into the ladies' toilet.

Ten minutes later she ventured out, and there were the three policemen waiting for her.

Without batting an eyelash, she said coyly, 'I'll bet you thought I wouldn't make it.'

An exhausted commercial traveller fell asleep at the wheel, and drove smack into the living-room of a roadside cottage. Embarrassed and humiliated, he climbed out of the car and mumbled, 'Can you tell me the way to the nearest garage?'

The householder said coldly, 'Straight ahead through the sideboard, and turn left at the piano.'

'What's the charge against this man?' asked the judge.

'Driving whilst having more than the permitted amount of alcohol in his system,' reported the policeman. 'He was fighting with the passenger in his car.'

'Bring in the passenger,' ordered the judge.

'That's just it, Your Honour,' said the policeman. 'There wasn't one.'

Mr. Smith took his wife and eight-year-old son out for a drive in his brand new car. He had an idea that, in his enthusiasm, he might exceed the speed limit, so he put his son on the back seat and told him to kneel up facing the rear.

'If you see a man in a blue uniform on a motor-cycle coming up from behind,' he told him, 'be sure to warn Daddy.'

Off they went, and the delighted Mr. Smith drove faster and faster. The speedometer had just registered 60 when the eight-year-old tapped his father on the shoulder.

'Daddy,' he reported, 'that gentleman you were expecting has arrived.'

A certain policeman who was always directing traffic near the office where Abey and Solly had their business was the bane of their lives. Every morning he would stop their cars and bawl them out unmercifully for some minor contravention of the Highway Code. Every lunchtime the partners worked themselves into a fine state of indignation over his behaviour.

One day Abey announced, 'Well, I finally told off that policeman this morning.'

Solly was deeply impressed. 'You didn't!' he said admiringly.

'Yes,' said Abey. 'I got so mad that I hardly knew what I was saying. "Who do you think you are?" I told him. "A general? A big boss? You seem to forget that you're nothing but a servant of the people. You are put at this spot to prevent accidents and direct traffic—not to insult taxpayers and peace-loving citizens who are going about their own business".'

'Wonderful! Wonderful!' breathed Solly. 'What did the policeman say?'

Abey sighed. 'He booked me.'

Little Jimmy came into the house crying his eyes out.

'What's the matter now?' asked his mother.

'Daddy was driving his new car out of the garage and he scratched the front wing,' said Jimmy.

'That's not so serious,' soothed his mother. 'A big boy like you shouldn't cry at a little thing like that. Why didn't you just laugh?'

'I did,' sobbed Jimmy.

Instructor: 'The hand-brake is put on in case of emergency.'

Lady Learner: 'Like a dressing-gown, you mean?'

The loudest noise known to man is the first rattle in your brand new car.

A motorist driving through the countryside found that the bridge over a stream had been washed away by a recent storm.

A local sat chewing a piece of straw by the side of the road.
'How deep is this stream?' asked the motorist.
'Dunno.'
'Do you think I can drive through it?'
'Why not?'
The motorist drove into the stream. His car promptly sank out of sight, and he himself barely got out with his life.
'What do you mean by telling me I could drive through that stream?' he asked furiously. 'It's eight feet deep if it's an inch!'
The native scratched his head. 'Can't understand it,' he admitted. 'The water only comes half-way up the ducks.'

A man walked into the showrooms of an exclusive motor dealers and said to the salesman, 'I'm thinking of buying a Rolls-Royce. Can you tell me the annual cost of running one, please?'
The salesman looked down his nose at the man and replied, 'Anybody who needs to ask a question like that, can't afford one.'

Then there was the story of the man who went up to the salesman at the Rolls-Royce stand at the Earls Court Motor Show and asked the way to the Gents' toilet.
The route was a bit complicated and the salesman deserted his post to escort the man to the door of the toilet.
Thanking him, the man asked why he had gone to so much trouble.
'Because,' answered the salesman, 'yours was the first genuine inquiry that I've had all day.'

A lady driving a small Continental car broke down in the high street. She didn't know the first thing about cars but thought that if she lifted the bonnet and pretended to tinker about, somebody would stop and help her.

When she opened the bonnet she was astonished to see that there was nothing there except the spare wheel!

Just at that moment, a friend of hers—another lady driving a similar model of car—pulled up behind her and asked what the trouble was.

'It's terrible!' said the first lady. 'My husband will go mad when he finds out. The engine has fallen out of my car. Look, there's nothing here at all!'

'Now, now,' consoled her friend. 'Don't get upset about it. I've got a spare engine in my boot. You can have that.'

'So your husband refused to buy you a car of your own?'

'He didn't exactly refuse. He said he thought I ought to become more familiar with machinery in general before I started driving. So he bought me a washing-machine to start on.'

A girl telephoned her boy-friend and said, 'You'd better not come over tonight. My father found out that we used his car to go out in last night, and he's mad.'

'How did he find out?'

'We hit him.'

'Do you know how to make your own anti-freeze?'

'Yes. Hide her winter woollies.'

Harry was telling his friend about a Christmas party he had attended.

'What fun! Everybody had a cracker with a present in it.'

'What did you get in yours?'

'A mini-car with automatic gears, a radio, disc brakes . . .'

'Just a minute. How could a car get into a cracker?'

'Easy. Woman driver.'

A husband went for a drive with his wife. She was a typical back-seat driver, and with every turn of the wheel she gave directions—'Go to the left.' 'Go to the right.' 'Mind that lorry.' 'Slow down a bit.' 'Watch these traffic lights.' Eventually, her husband could stand it no longer.

He drove to where he knew there was a level-crossing, timing his arrival to be about ten seconds before an express train was due to cross. He drove the car on to the railway line and stopped.

Then, jumping quickly out of the car and slamming the door, he shouted, 'I got my end over. What are you going to do about yours?'

A man met a friend who was all bandaged up.

'What happened?' he asked.

'I was driving in heavy traffic and another car bumped into me from the back. I got out and we had a terrific argument. He broke my nose, blacked my eye and knocked my teeth out.'

'Why didn't you call a policeman?'

'He was a policeman.'

A businessman had a great time at the office party, had a slight accident while driving home and, thanks to the breathaliser, lost his driving licence.

Fortunately his wife had a licence and was able to take him to and from the office. One day, she was speeding along at about 50 mph when a motor-cycle policeman overtook her and signalled her to stop.

Taking out his notebook, he looked down at her and said, 'I'm going to put you down for fifty-five.'

She turned to her husband and said, 'That proves it. I told you this hat made me look old!'

A motorist who had been in a car accident which wasn't his fault, had to walk round on crutches. Some months later, a friend asked him how he was getting on.

'Not so bad,' he admitted. 'In fact, my doctor says I don't need the crutches now. But my solicitor says that I do.'

A man took his wife and his mother-in-law out for a drive. His mother-in-law sat in the back seat and 'drove' the car from there. The driver's wife noticed that he was getting madder and madder.

'Ignore her,' she whispered to her husband. 'She's her own worst enemy.'

'Not while I'm alive,' he muttered back.

Two cars crashed into each other. One driver was unharmed but the other staggered out of his car in a dazed condition.

The driver who wasn't hurt, and whose fault the crash had

been, quickly got a flask of brandy out of his pocket and forced some between the other's lips, saying, 'Here you are, old man. This will make you feel better.'

A policeman arrived on the scene, just as the brandy had aided the man's recovery, and asked who was to blame.

The unscathed driver pointed to the other and said, 'Smell his breath.'

The owner of a large seaside car-park called all his attendants into his office and told them: 'We haven't had a single complaint about a scratched or dented car all week. How can I make any money when you're leaving so much space?'

Bill: 'I've worked out a way of ensuring that young Dickie isn't late for grammar school in the mornings.'

Brian: 'What is it?'

Bill: 'I've bought him a car.'

Brian: 'How does that help?'

Bill: 'He's got to get there early to find a parking place.'

Free Advice: Never drive a car when you're drunk. It's hard enough to get the pedestrian you're after when you're sober.

'What happened to the car?'

'I bumped into a cow.'

'Was it a Jersey cow?'

'I don't know. Didn't see its number plate.'

A man was speeding down a winding country lane and failed to negotiate a curve. His car crashed into a fence and then rolled over several times.

A farmer who saw the occurrence ran over as the driver crawled out of the wreckage and asked, 'Are you drunk?'

'Of course I'm drunk,' answered the motorist. 'What do you think I am—a stunt driver?'

The driver's wife looked at the road map and said, 'Darling, I'm not trying to interfere, but we're going in the wrong direction.'

'So what?' he answered. 'We're making great time.'

'Does your wife drive?'

'No. My car was like this when I bought it.'

When a man opens the door of his car for his wife, you can be sure that either the car or the wife is new.

Lost in countryside while trying to take a short cut, a motorist stopped beside an elderly farmhand who was walking along the road.

'Can you tell me the way to the next town?' he asked.

'Certainly,' answered the farmhand. 'You turn right at the next junction and go along that road until you come to a red farmhouse. Turn right again until you come to a pub called

'The Swan and Cemetery', then go right to the A.A. box. Then turn left.'

Twenty minutes later, the same car came along the same road and pulled up alongside the same farmhand.

'I never could follow directions properly,' said the motorist. 'I wonder if you'd be good enough to get in and direct me?'

'Yes,' said the farmhand, climbing in. 'Just go straight ahead. Sometimes I send drivers round two or three times before they offer me a ride.'

A salesman overtook a young man running along the road. He stopped and invited the perspiring runner to get in.

'An emergency, I suppose?' the driver asked.

'No,' puffed the young man. 'I always run like that when I want a lift. It seldom fails.'

'I've come back to buy that car you showed me yesterday,' the man said as he stepped into the car showrooms.

'That's fine,' said the salesman, 'I thought you'd be back. As a matter of interest, what was the dominant feature that made you decide to buy this car?'

'The wife.'

A doctor asked his patient, 'Why have you got JBA 2E tattooed in reverse on your back?'

'That's not a tattoo,' was the reply. 'That's where my wife ran into me when I was opening the garage doors.'

An old and battered car stopped outside an exclusive restaurant. The driver went up to a man who was standing nearby and asked, 'Will you keep an eye on my car while I make a phone call?'

The man agreed, and when the driver returned he asked how much he owed him for his services.

'Ten pounds,' was the reply.

'But that's daylight robbery. I was only away for five minutes.'

'I know,' the man replied. 'But it wasn't the time, it was the embarrassment. Everyone thought it was my car.'

If all the motorists in the country were laid end to end, ninety-nine per cent of them would immediately pull out of line and try to pass the car in front.

It takes over 2,000 *bolts and screws to assemble a car—but it only takes one nut to scatter it all over the road.*

A woman, trying to reverse into a parking space, smashed into the car behind. Moving forward, she smashed into the car in front. Then, she recklessly pulled out of the space and hit a passing car.

A policeman who had been watching her came over.

'Can I see your licence, please?' he asked.

'Oh, don't be silly,' she snapped. 'Who'd give me a licence?'

A motorist who had broken down on a quiet country road opened the bonnet and inspected the engine.

'The trouble's in the battery,' came a voice from behind him.

The motorist turned round, but the only thing in sight was a horse watching him from a field. This completely un-nerved the man and he set off down the road. After about ten minutes, he came to a garage and told his story to the owner.

'You mean to say that there was nobody near the car except a horse?' asked the garage proprietor.

'That's right.'

'Was it by any chance a white horse with a black patch on its head?'

'Yes, it was.'

'Well, ignore him. He doesn't know a thing about cars.'

He (stopping on a country road)*:* 'The petrol's run out.'

She (taking a whisky bottle from her handbag)*:* 'Look what I've got.'

He: 'A full bottle of whisky! What kind is it?'

She: 'Esso Extra.'

Study in mixed emotions: the man who saw his mother-in-law go over a cliff in his brand new Jaguar.

Magistrate: 'The officer says you were doing 50 mph.'

Motorist: 'I wasn't even doing thirty. In fact, I wasn't doing twenty, or even ten.'

Magistrate: 'Fined £5 for illegal parking.'

A man lost control of his car and ran into a telegraph pole. When he regained consciousness, he found himself lying on several telephone wires that he had brought down.

'Thank goodness,' he sighed. 'It's a harp.'

A vain young woman had persuaded her boy-friend to give her driving lessons. Climbing into the driving-seat for the first time, she said, 'Donald, darling, the little mirror up here isn't set right.'

'It is dear. It must be, because we're the same height.'

'Well, someobody must have moved it,' insisted the young lady. 'I can't see myself in it. All I can see are the cars behind us.'

The village parson rebuked the husband for spending so much time tinkering with his car.

'If I were you,' he said, 'I'd put my wife before my car.'

'I'd like to,' sighed the man. 'But I'm afraid somebody might catch me at it.'

The weary husband had just dug a fifty-yard path from his garage to the road through a six-foot snow drift.

As he was about to open the garage door, with an obvious air of triumph, his dear little wife called out from the kitchen, 'Oh, I forgot to tell you, darling. I took the car over to mother's yesterday before the snow started.'

The newspaper that printed this report of an accident shall remain nameless. *When the car overturned both girls were injured; Miss X about the face, and Miss Y in the back seat.*

Announcement from the stage: 'Will the owner of the car with the zebra-skin upholstery please go outside immediately? A beserk donkey is assaulting his back seat.'

A timid motorist, caught in the fog, decided to take the easy way out and followed closely behind the car in front. This worked fine until the car that was guiding him stopped short, and the timid driver didn't!

He realised that the crash was his fault, but he used the time-honoured way out and asked the other driver, 'Why don't you stick your hand out and give a signal when you're going to stop?'

'In my own garage?' was the unexpected reply.

Patrick O'Reilly bought a high-powered sports car and asked a priest to give it his blessing.

The priest agreed, but cautioned, 'Remember, Patrick, that this blessing is no good above forty miles an hour.'

A motor-cycle policeman spotted a car being driven well over the speed limit in a built-up area, and gave chase. Stopping the car, the policeman was surprised to see that the driver was his own parish priest.

'I'm dreadfully sorry,' apologised the priest. 'It's a brand new car and I didn't realise how fast I was going.'

'I'll let you go this time, Father,' grinned the policeman. 'Provided you say ten Hail Marys and fifteen Our Fathers.'

'Did you hear about Roger? He was a hundred yards from an open railway crossing and travelling at 70 miles an hour. A train, coming down the line at 80 miles an hour, was just over a hundred yards from the intersection.'

'Good heavens! Did he get across?'

'Oh, yes—a marble one that his widow bought with the insurance money.'

A hen-pecked husband was driving his wife and her friend into town.

The wife's friend asked, 'Why does your husband always put his hand out when he's driving?'

The wife answered, 'I suppose it's because the worm is getting ready to turn.'

Lady: 'What's your name?'

New Chauffeur: 'Benjamin, madam.'

Lady (haughtily)*:* 'I always address my chauffeurs by their surname. What is it?'

New Chauffeur: 'Darling, madam.'

Lady: 'Drive on, Benjamin.'

A small red sports car was speeding along a country lane when a tractor pulled out of a field twenty yards ahead. Unable to stop in time, the driver of the sports car thought quickly and drove off the road, through the hedge, and into the field. The driver of the tractor mopped his brow and muttered, 'Blimey, I only just got out of that field in time!'

* * *

In certain parts of the United States of America 'traffic regulators'—as they are called there—have noticed that motorists seem to regard the hundreds of conventional road signs as part of the scenery, and that they are more likely to be slowed down to a mere 70 miles an hour by such signs as:

DRIVE CAREFULLY. DON'T INSIST ON YOUR RITES.

* * *

SEVENTY-THREE PEOPLE DIED HERE LAST YEAR FROM GAS. TWO INHALED IT, FOUR PUT A LIGHTED MATCH TO IT, AND SIXTY-SEVEN STEPPED ON IT.

* * *

GO SLOW—THIS IS A ONE HEARSE TOWN.

THE AVERAGE TIME IT TAKES A TRAIN TO PASS THIS CROSSING IS TWELVE SECONDS—WHETHER YOUR CAR IS ON IT OR NOT.

* * *

CROSSROADS: BETTER HUMOUR THEM.

* * *

A scrap-iron merchant with premises near a busy level-crossing consolingly advertises:

GO AHEAD AND TAKE A CHANCE. WE'LL BUY WHAT'S LEFT OF YOUR CAR.

* * *

While a warning posted at the entrance to a frequently-flooded country road reads:

TAKE NOTICE. WHEN THIS SIGN IS UNDER WATER, THE ROAD IS IMPASSABLE.

* * *

Famous last words: 'So he won't dip his headlights, eh? Then I'm darned if I'll dip mine.'

'I've had this car for twenty years and never had a wreck.'
'Haven't you got that the wrong way round?'

A scoutmaster stopped his car at a zebra crossing, and a very plain, gawky, badly-dressed girl crossed the road looking as miserable as it is possible for a human being to look.

The scoutmaster leaned out of his car, gave the girl a wolf-whistle, and beckoned to her. The girl looked shocked and ran to the pavement.

The scoutmaster drove on, murmuring happily, 'Well, that's my good deed for today.'

First Motorist: 'My wife tells me that you nearly bumped into her when she was crossing the road yesterday.'

Second Motorist: 'Did I? I'm very sorry. Have a go at mine next time you see her.'

It takes a woman motorist longer to dress than it does a man because she has to slow down for the curves.

A motorist is a man who, after seeing a bad crash, drives carefully for the next half mile.

'You've no rear-light showing,' said the policeman to a motorist late one night. 'I shall have to ask you for your driving-licence, please.'

The motorist got out to investigate, and let out a wail of dismay.

'Oh, no!' he cried. 'It can't be! It's impossible! This is going to cost me a fortune! The wife'll go mad!'

'Come now,' said the policeman. 'It's not as serious as all that.'

The motorist explained, 'It's not the rear light that's worrying me. Where's my caravan gone?'

'I was almost killed twice in a car.'
'Once would have been enough.'

'A steamroller ran over my uncle.'
'What did you do?'
'I just took him home and slipped him under the door.'

'If you hugged the curve, you should have been safe.'
'It wasn't that kind of curve.'

Impressed by an advertisement offering 'A year's supply of free petrol to anybody buying a used car from us', a man went along to where they were being sold. A keen young salesman showed him some cars, but they were well past their best and the man refused to bite. Aware that the boss was watching him, the salesman didn't give up, but the man still said 'No'.

At this point, the boss took over, showed the man a car and made a sale in two minutes flat.

As the customer drove out in his car, the boss said, 'You see how easy it is when you know how? He bought the first car that I showed him.'

'Yes,' agreed the salesman. 'But who made him dizzy?'

Policeman: 'How did you come to hit that telegraph pole?'
Woman Driver: 'Would you believe self-defence?'

A policeman was visiting a motorist in hospital to obtain a statement from him.

'Now, tell me, slowly and in your own words, what happened,' he said.

'Well,' the motorist began, 'I was driving along this narrow road and a car was coming towards me at 60 miles an hour, so I moved over to let him pass. Then I saw another car doing the same thing, so I moved over to let that one pass. Then another car, and another. Then I saw a bridge coming towards me, so I moved over to let it pass, and that's all I remember.'

Magistrate: 'The officer says that you were very sarcastic to him after he had pulled you up for speeding.'

Motorist: 'I didn't intend to be. But he lectured me so much like my wife does that I forgot myself and kept saying, 'Yes dear'.'

'What a terrible accident. It's a wonder your neck wasn't broken.'

'Well, it was interrupted.'

An optimist is a man who thinks his wife can drive a five-foot-wide car through a ten-foot-wide gateway.

It takes some people as long as three cars to learn to drive.

A man driving along a country road pulled up in answer to a signal from a lady motorist.

'I've got a flat tyre,' she told him. 'I ran over a bottle about half a mile back.'

'Couldn't you see it and avoid it?' asked the man.

'Of course I couldn't. The silly fool had it in his pocket.'

A girl and a car are much alike. A good paint job hides the years, but the lines tell the story.

'You were doing 45 miles an hour,' the policeman told the motorist he had pulled up.

The lady sitting in the passenger seat cackled gleefully, 'Book him, officer. It just serves him right. I've been telling him for years that he's a reckless, dangerous, inconsiderate driver.'

'Your wife?' queried the policeman. When the driver nodded glumly, he snapped his notebook shut and added, 'Drive on, brother. Drive on!'

Sunday Drivers

EVERY SUNDAY, every summer, I have had to drive from whichever seaside town I am appearing in to a holiday camp some 120 miles away. It's my living and I have to do it, otherwise I wouldn't stray from my own garden. That way, I would avoid the biggest menace on the road—The Sunday Driver. I know it isn't YOU, dear reader. But you know the chap I mean, don't you?.

I am convinced that they are sent out from a central office. One for every road in the country. I am equally convinced that they are issued with a set of rules which they have to obey. I haven't actually seen the list, but I should imagine it reads as follows:

1. Always remember to fill the car with the largest number of children, aunts, uncles and in-laws that you can cram in.

2. Always drive at 5 mph less than the permitted limit, and *never* exceed 40 mph on any road.

3. Always take up a position on the road which prohibits any other vehicle from overtaking you. (If somebody should

manage to get past you, blast your horn and tell your passengers what an idiot the other driver is.)

4. When turning right at traffic lights, take up a position in the outside lane but do not give any indication that you are turning right until the lights change to green. This will ensure that there is at least one car (more if you're lucky) behind you who wants to drive straight on and thought that you were.

5. Ask one of the people sat on the back seat to glance back occasionally and count the number of cars that you are holding up. Remember there is a prize for the driver who collects the most. This week's prize is a 'We've seen the Penguins at Poshsea' sticker to add to the others which cover your rear window.

6. If possible, take up a position immediately behind a slow-moving heavy-goods vehicle and slightly to his off-side. Give the appearance of trying to overtake it, but *never* do so.

7. All drivers are requested to take a card-table, some folding chairs and a picnic hamper in order that they can sit at the roadside until the evening.

8. Do not commence your return journey until the traffic is at its busiest.

Announcement flashed on cinema screen: 'Will the owner of car number SFR3968492635386749H please go outside. His car's all right, but the number-plate is blocking the car park exit.'

Hearing the car behind him hooting loudly, the driver of a large American car glanced into his rear view mirror and saw a small, battered pre-war saloon dangerously close to him. Accelerating rapidly to sixty miles an hour in order to leave the small car behind, he again glanced into the mirror and was astonished to see that it was still on his tail and the driver was still banging away on the horn. Increasing his speed to well over a hundred miles an hour did no good at all – the small car kept with him.

By this time, the driver of the large car was slightly annoyed and he pulled in at the side of the road in order to let the other driver pass him. However, the small car pulled in right behind him and its driver got out.

Approaching the other driver, he breathed a sigh of relief and said, 'Thank goodness you've stopped – my front bumper has been caught on your rear bumper for the last five miles.'

'Harry's car doesn't use any petrol.'

'How can that be?'

'Don't ask me, but it's true. Last night he went forty miles out of his way to take a girl home from the dance, and when I saw him this morning he said, "All that way for nothing".'

The trouble with bucket seats in cars is that not everyone has the same sized bucket.

A young man was giving a lift to a pretty hitch-hiker when he said, "I can hear a knocking sound. I wonder what it is?'

'I don't know,' replied the modern miss. 'But I can tell you one thing for sure – it isn't opportunity.'

The windows of the car parked in a lay-by late one dark night were well and truly steamed up when the couple on the back seat heard the voice of the law outside the car saying, 'Hello, hello, hello . . . what's going on here, then?'

The policeman opened the car door, gave the couple a two-minute lecture about the laws of the country and then shone his torch on them as he informed them that he was going to report them.

'But officer,' protested the man, 'this lady is my wife. I was driving along the road in the pouring rain when I saw her walking along with a raincoat over her head. So I stopped to pick her up, and after a while we pulled in here to have a rest.'

'Then why on earth didn't you tell me it was your wife instead of letting me lecture you?' the policeman demanded.

'Well,' said the man, 'I didn't know it *was* until you shone your torch on her.'

'If a policeman stops you for a motoring offence, answer him back and show him who's boss!' was Tommy's motto.

A policeman stopped him once for driving through traffic lights when they were on red, and said, 'Didn't you see those traffic lights on red?'

'Yes,' answered Tommy.

'Well, why didn't you stop?'

'Because when you've seen one, you've seen them all!'

And the policeman went away.

And Tommy went with him . . .

Two hippies, a boy and a girl, were driving along in an old 'banger' when the engine stalled as they were going downhill. Stopping at the side of the road, the youth persuaded his girlfriend to join him underneath the car, on the pretext that two would be able to find the fault quicker than one.

Some twenty minutes later they were locked in a passionate embrace when a policeman tapped the youth on the shoulder and asked what he was doing.

'Like, I'm fixing the clutch, man,' replied the hippie.

'Well, while you're about it, you'd better fix the brakes,' said the policeman. 'Your car rolled down the hill ten minutes ago.'

The middle-aged couple in the family saloon had been tailed by the smart white sports car for several miles before it finally overtook them. Then, long fair hair streaming in the wind, the driver swung the car out, accelerated and roared away into the distance.

'You know, I was sure that driver was a girl until that car overtook us,' the wife then said with a smile.

'What do you mean?' queried the husband. 'It *was* a girl, wasn't it?'

'No. I got a closer look as the car went past. It was definitely a young fellow with long hair.'

There was a moment's pause. Then the husband said sheepishly, 'In that case, I wish I hadn't winked.'